THE ULTIMATE RELATIONSHIP
JOURNAL FOR COUPLES

THE ULTIMATE RELATIONSHIP JOURNAL

FOR COUPLES

PROMPTS AND PRACTICES TO CONNECT AND STRENGTHEN YOUR BOND

MIRIAM TORRES BRINKMANN, PhD, LMFT

ROCKRIDGE
PRESS

To Peter, you're my blue sky, you're my sunny day

Interior and Cover Designer: Monica Cheng
Art Producer: Sara Feinstein
Editor: Nora Spiegel
Production Manager: Riley Hoffman
Production Editor: Melissa Edeburn

Illustration used under license from Vector Stock. Author photo courtesy of Chelsea V Photography.

Paperback ISBN: 978-1-63807-378-9

This Journal Belongs to:

_____

and

_____

Contents

Introduction

So, why a journal?

There is something extremely transformative in the process of sharing your thoughts, feelings, and ideas, not to mention your perspective on past experiences, through writing. In all my years as a couples therapist and relationship coach, I have seen for myself how effective and powerful journaling, the simple act of "writing it out," can be. I'm certain both you and your partner will find this guided journal to be an empowering experience.

Multiple research studies show a strong correlation between journaling and well-being, both psychological and physical. Writing helps remove our mental blocks, and it can clarify our thoughts and feelings. The writing process slows down the mind, so both the emotional and logical sides of our brain can express themselves with more intention. Journaling induces a kind of introspection that is difficult to achieve any other way.

The prompts, practices, and quotes in these pages will guide you to explore each other's narratives with openness and loving curiosity. Any committed couple can benefit from this book, from the newly dating pair to those celebrating their golden anniversary, gay or straight, and formally married or longtime companions. I've chosen content that will help couples in all phases of a relationship. Whatever state your partnership is in, this journal will empower you to improve communication and get to know your partner—and even yourself—more profoundly.

Another advantage to journaling is its inherent flexibility. You can approach this journal any way you wish. You might devote a whole weekend to a self-created couples retreat and really dig in. Or you can choose an interesting or promising prompt when you both have the time. You can work from the front of the book to the back, but there is no mandated sequence to follow. You can randomly open to any page and follow its lead, or search for a topic you that resonates with you.

But do remember, although this journal can be a great supplement to therapy or counseling, it is not a replacement for professional help. Don't hesitate to seek a couples therapist if you think you need some external guidance. See the Resources at the end of this book (page 158) if you need help finding a therapist.

You'll see that the contents of this book are grouped into five broad relationship topics. Within each section, you'll find prompts to guide your journal writing, practices to do together, and cogent quotes to reflect upon and inspire you in these activities.

However you choose to embark on this journey, I invite you and your partner to explore together, bringing an open heart and a loving mind.

Quick-Start Guide

➥ If you and your partner are interested in exploring your emotional needs, roles, and communication styles or learning how to deal with potentially sensitive topics, I suggest you go straight to section 1, "Our Story" (page 1).

➥ If your biggest priority is to learn about trust, vulnerability, and boundaries, jump right into section 2, "In Us We Trust" (page 31).

➥ If resolving conflict is your Achilles' heel, look no further than section 3, "Conflict" (page 63), where you can explore discord, triggers, negative emotions, and forgiveness.

➥ Section 4, "Family Matters" (page 93), will help you navigate issues like family dynamics, parenting, family values, and loss and grief.

➥ If you and your partner are ready to relight the spark and explore your intimate and erotic landscapes, go to section 5, "Sex and Intimacy" (page 125).

How to Use This Journal with
The Ultimate Relationship Workbook for Couples

The goal of this journal is to provide couples with tools to help in the care and nurturing of their relationship. To that end, this book is a companion to *The Ultimate Relationship Workbook for Couples*, which is organized in the same way and covers a very similar range of topics. Although similar to the workbook in subject matter, this journal is quite different in its application. Whereas the workbook has written exercises, guided conversations, and takeaways, this journal combines writing prompts with activities to try and quotes to reflect on.

If the *Ultimate Relationship Workbook for Couples* isn't currently on your bookshelf, don't worry! This journal can be used as a stand-alone resource for relationships at any stage. If you've already read the workbook and you're looking for more guidance to go deeper, you will find it here. If you're just getting started with the workbook, you can work through both books together, alternating between the matching sections in each.

And if you are in, or thinking about, couples therapy, this journal can be a resource to use in conjunction with professional help. But remember, no book is a substitute for therapy.

The Ground Rules

To ensure that you get the most out of this journal, it's important to establish some ground rules. Here are some fundamental ones, but feel free to add to the list.

1. **Take turns with the prompts.** You'll see that the book is designed with room for each partner to answer the writing prompts in turn. One of you should be assigned as Partner A and the other as Partner B (perhaps alternate who gets to go first). If you write second, I suggest covering your partner's answer, so you'll write your own thoughts without being influenced by their response.

2. **Use the prompts as a starting point.** Once you've both completed a writing prompt, your work is only half done! Review each other's responses and talk through them.

3. **Always show respect and compassion.** Getting the most out of this endeavor requires that you each lower some of your barriers and open up to your vulnerabilities. For that to be possible, respect and compassion for each other need to be at the forefront.

4. **Start with intention.** A ritual is a good way to signal to your brain and your heart that it's time to open up. Your ritual doesn't have to be elaborate; for example, light a candle, make a pot of tea, turn your phone off, or turn on some inspiring music.

5. **Stay open, curious, and nonjudgmental.** For the magic of this book to happen, avoid defining, judging, or dismissing your partner's experiences or feelings. Don't say things like "you are too sensitive," or "you shouldn't feel that way." Instead, ask questions.

6. **Remember, this is teamwork.** Commit to approaching these conversations and exercises as a team. Take turns picking topics and managing the process.

7. **Don't dodge the issues.** You might not agree with each other on certain topics, and that's OK. The key is that both partners feel heard and validated (even when you disagree). If a topic appears especially difficult, affirm your respect and compassion . . . and jump into it. Trust that you can navigate every topic in this book!

We come to love not by finding a perfect person, but by learning to see an imperfect person perfectly.

SAM KEEN, AUTHOR AND PHILOSOPHER

1
OUR STORY

These prompts and exercises will help you tell the story of your relationship: the roles you play, the ways you communicate, what you value, and your love for each other. The goal is to explore your connection and the love story you have formed together. The greater your understanding of what makes your relationship unique and special, the stronger your bond—and the greater your ability to recover from setbacks life throws your way.

Describe what qualities you most admire about your partner. Why are those qualities meaningful for you? If some of these qualities make your life better, please elaborate. How do you feel when you perceive your partner exhibiting one of these qualities?

Partner A

_____

_____

_____

_____

_____

_____

_____

Partner B

_____

_____

_____

_____

_____

_____

_____

Without thinking too hard about it, jot down a few words about what love means to you. Then describe in more detail how you show love to your partner, and how your partner shows love to you.

Partner A

_____

_____

_____

_____

_____

_____

Partner B

_____

_____

_____

_____

_____

_____

Think about a time when you felt most connected to your partner. Why did you feel that way? What physical sensations did you have? What thoughts were feeding that connection? What could you do today (note that this is about YOU, not your partner) to re-create those feelings of connection?

Partner A

_____

_____

_____

_____

_____

_____

Partner B

_____

_____

_____

_____

_____

_____

GRATITUDE JOURNAL

Gratitude is an essential part of a happy life and a happy relationship. There cannot be joy without a feeling of gratitude. Get together with your partner and share at least 10 things that are good in your life right now: One partner names something, then the other names something else, alternating until you get to 10 each (or keep going for as long as you'd like). Then, over the course of the following seven days, create a gratitude journal. In a notebook or by whatever method you choose, document what you're grateful for regarding your partner and your relationship. At least once a day, share these thoughts and feelings with each other. You can send text messages or pictures, leave notes, or— the best option—get together and read your notes to each other. The more detail, the better.

A relationship role is a pattern of behaviors we all fall into. They can be logistical (household roles, for example), social (who makes all the social plans?), or emotional (perhaps you're the "emotional" or "logical" one). In the space provided, list all the relationship roles each of you plays in your relationship.

Partner A

_____

_____

_____

_____

_____

_____

Partner B

_____

_____

_____

_____

_____

_____

Looking at the list of roles from the previous prompt, which do you enjoy most?
Which do you feel most burdened by? Can you identify any values, needs, desires,
or emotions at the root of the roles you play? For example, if you are the one who
always cooks, that might be because healthy food is an important value for you.

Partner A

_____

_____

_____

_____

_____

_____

Partner B

_____

_____

_____

_____

_____

_____

EMOTIONAL BANK ACCOUNT

The relationship researcher John Gottman has said that we need to have an emotional bank account with a positive balance. Any negative interactions act like a withdrawal from the emotional bank account, at an exchange rate of 5:1, meaning it takes a deposit of five positive experiences to make up for one negative. With that in mind, each of you take out a pen and paper and list at least five ways your partner can fill up your bank account. Then write at least five ways you could fill up your partner's bank account. For example, things that commonly fill up emotional bank accounts are acknowledging your partner's comments by vocalizing or nodding or smiling, looking into their eyes when they talk, holding their hand, and kissing hello and goodbye. Compare notes and discuss when you're done making your lists.

Emotional needs are conditions or feelings that we need to fulfill in order to feel happy or satisfied. Make an inventory of your emotional needs. Examples include affection, trust, sexual fulfillment, companionship, and commitment. Then write down what you feel when those needs are not met and how, or if, you communicate those needs to your partner.

Partner A

_____

_____

_____

_____

_____

_____

Partner B

_____

_____

_____

_____

_____

_____

What do you wish your partner knew or understood about your needs when you are under stress? What would be the ideal way for you to communicate those needs during stressful moments?

Partner A

_____

_____

_____

_____

_____

_____

Partner B

_____

_____

_____

_____

_____

_____

Imagine your relationship is a living being that needs attention and nourishment. How can you best provide that nourishment so this being not only stays healthy but thrives? Does it grow when you're kind to your partner or when you spend time together? Does it weaken if you don't turn your phone off after a certain hour?

Partner A

_____

_____

_____

_____

_____

_____

Partner B

_____

_____

_____

_____

_____

_____

SAVORING THE MOMENT

Happiness research shows that savoring the moment plays a big part in well-being. When we are aware of the moment and appreciate and intensify the positive emotions as they happen, we are savoring the moment. For this activity, pick a day to spend together during which both of you will consciously savor every moment, every taste, and every interaction as if it were the most special thing ever. Check in with each other frequently; if one of you loses focus, don't judge—just get back to the activity. If a day feels too long for this exercise, try starting with half a day. This practice can require some brain training, but it's worth it. And you have each other to help stay focused on the savoring the moment!

Supporting each other's dreams is essential for a healthy relationship. Write down five of your own life dreams and what your partner can do to support each of them. Then list five of your partner's dreams and describe how you can support them.

Partner A

_____

_____

_____

_____

_____

_____

_____

Partner B

_____

_____

_____

_____

_____

_____

_____

Deep friendship is a core element of a happy relationship. Describe what makes your partner a good friend and what makes you a good friend to your partner.

Partner A

_____

_____

_____

_____

_____

_____

_____

Partner B

_____

_____

_____

_____

_____

_____

_____

A good relationship will necessarily entail a lot of accepting and compromising—in other words, embracing your differences. What are the things you believe your partner accepts in you and what are the things that you accept about your partner?

Partner A

_____

_____

_____

_____

_____

_____

_____

Partner B

_____

_____

_____

_____

_____

_____

_____

Listen with curiosity. Speak with honesty. Act with integrity. The greatest problem with communication is we don't listen to understand. We listen to reply. When we listen with curiosity, we don't listen with the intent to reply. We listen for what's behind the words.

ROY T. BENNETT, AUTHOR

Good communication is crucial to a healthy relationship. But not all topics are easy to talk about. Make a list of a few topics that you find difficult to discuss with your partner. Briefly explain why each one is difficult, and how you'd like your partner to respond when you open up about it.

Partner A

_____

_____

_____

_____

_____

_____

_____

Partner B

_____

_____

_____

_____

_____

_____

_____

How would you best describe your communication style, and how is it different from your partner's communication style? Considering your family history, can you identify where and why you learned or developed your style of communicating?

Partner A

_____

_____

_____

_____

_____

_____

_____

Partner B

_____

_____

_____

_____

_____

_____

_____

When there's a disagreement or difficulty between you two, what is your default reaction? Do you become defensive, try to debate, or try to change the subject? How would you like to react instead to create a more loving interaction?

Partner A

_____

_____

_____

_____

_____

_____

_____

Partner B

_____

_____

_____

_____

_____

_____

_____

BIGGEST FEARS

Fear is a primary emotion that's behind many other feelings, like anger or anxiety. It's important to know and understand your own fears as well as your partner's fears. Find some time together, without interruptions, for a heart-to-heart conversation about this. Ask each other the following questions:

1. What is your greatest fear?
2. What is a fear that you have never told me about?
3. How would your life be different if you didn't have that fear?
4. How can we be more open with each other about what we're afraid of?

If you were to die unexpectedly, what would you most like to be remembered for by your partner? If the situation were reversed, how would you like to remember your partner?

Partner A

_____

_____

_____

_____

_____

_____

_____

Partner B

_____

_____

_____

_____

_____

_____

_____

Research shows that positive reminiscence in couples can help improve communication. Imagine you are writing a movie script about your relationship. Describe how you met your partner, how the relationship developed, and how the love blossomed.

Partner A

_____

_____

_____

_____

_____

_____

_____

Partner B

_____

_____

_____

_____

_____

_____

_____

While you were growing up, what was your family's attitude toward money, and how similar is that to your current attitude? What's financially important to you, and why? How similar or different do you perceive your partner's attitude toward money to be, compared to yours?

Partner A

_____

_____

_____

_____

_____

_____

_____

Partner B

_____

_____

_____

_____

_____

_____

_____

How would you define your social life as a couple? How important are your "outside" relationships to you? Do you like the level and style of contact you currently have with other people, or would you like to change something? Are you aligned with your partner on this topic?

Partner A

_____

_____

_____

_____

_____

_____

_____

Partner B

_____

_____

_____

_____

_____

_____

_____

CORE VALUES

The goal of this exercise is to take a close look at your life choices and see if they align with your values. Sharing common values is a strong indicator of happiness in a relationship. When we speak of core values, we're not talking about hobbies or interests, but the deep-rooted convictions that guide your life. Think about how you spend your time and money, and what you consider to be most inspiring or enjoyable for you. Doing so will give you an idea of what your core values are. Examples include being a good parent, staying healthy and fit, traveling regularly, spending time with family, and being financially successful. For this practice, get a sheet of paper and make a list of your core values, taking turns to write one value at a time. Afterward, discuss why those values are important to each of you.

What do religion and spirituality mean to you? Is there anything you would like your partner to know or understand about your religious and spiritual values?

Partner A

_____

_____

_____

_____

_____

_____

Partner B

_____

_____

_____

_____

_____

_____

In a relationship, we take it for granted that our partner sees the world the same way we do—and therefore wants the same things, whether it's how many kids to have or where to live or how to spend or save money.

LOGAN URY,
AUTHOR AND BEHAVIORAL SCIENTIST

Having the same interests is not as important as having the same outlook on life. How is your attitude on life similar to, or different from, your partner's? Do you think that both of you want the same things over the long term? What are those things?

Partner A

_____

_____

_____

_____

_____

_____

Partner B

_____

_____

_____

_____

_____

_____

IDEAL DAY

How would you describe your ideal day? Taking turns, each of you describe to the other in detail the features in your personal ideal day. Allow yourselves to dream—this is the day when you can do whatever you want. Then take all the common denominators in each of your ideal days and design your perfect day together. Make a plan for the next time you both have time off to create a day that resembles this collaborative creation. If part of this dream day requires you to be somewhere else in the world, just try to re-create as much as you can for now.

I'm never more courageous than when I'm embracing imperfection, embracing vulnerabilities, and setting boundaries with the people in my life.

BRENÉ BROWN,
AUTHOR AND RESEARCH PROFESSOR

2

IN US WE TRUST

How can we be in a relationship without losing our
individuality? Do we trust each other? What is the
difference between secrecy and privacy? What are
realistic and fair boundaries? In this section, we will
explore common questions and issues related to
trust. Remember that every relationship is unique,
so there are no absolute right or wrong answers.
Rather, working through these issues together will
help you come up with answers of your own.

Think about what trust means to you in the context of your relationship. With that in mind, write five different endings to this sentence: "I completely trust my partner to_____." Add more if you are inspired!

Partner A

_____

_____

_____

_____

_____

_____

Partner B

_____

_____

_____

_____

_____

_____

The most trusting partners are those who can be confident that their loved one has their best interest at heart. Describe how you and your partner put each other's best interest at the forefront.

Partner A

_____

_____

_____

_____

_____

_____

_____

Partner B

_____

_____

_____

_____

_____

_____

_____

TRUTH OR DARE

Take turns choosing between answering a question truthfully or performing a dare. No changes of mind are allowed.

If your partner chooses truth, ask a question to which you want a truthful answer. Remember that this is an opportunity for building trust. Some suggestions:

- What's your favorite place to make love?
- What's your most embarrassing moment?
- When was last time you laughed really hard?

If your partner chooses dare, they're giving you a chance to ask for a romantic gesture, so give them a (perhaps silly) task that shows their love. It might be to

- Sing a romantic song.
- Post on social media the five things you love most about me.
- Vacuum the living room wearing only your underwear.

How does it feel when you think about your partner being there for you during a challenging or stressful time in your life? Recount an episode when your partner had your back, and how that made you feel.

Partner A

_____

_____

_____

_____

_____

_____

_____

Partner B

_____

_____

_____

_____

_____

_____

_____

There are many different facets of trust: emotional, financial, sexual, and so on. Has anyone ever broken your trust in the past? Describe what happened. How did that affect how trusting you are now?

Partner A

_____

_____

_____

_____

_____

_____

_____

Partner B

_____

_____

_____

_____

_____

_____

_____

There's a difference between *privacy*, the right to be left alone, and *secrecy*, hiding information because of shame or fear of the consequences. Privacy is consensual and healthy in a relationship. Secrecy breaks trust. Can you think of some real-life or hypothetical examples of both privacy and secrecy? What boundaries have the two of you established around sharing and transparency? Do you feel that those boundaries are respected?

Partner A

_____

_____

_____

_____

_____

_____

Partner B

_____

_____

_____

_____

_____

_____

What does *fidelity* mean to you? What are the sexual and emotional boundaries in your relationship? What would you consider to be an affair or a breach of trust?

Partner A

_____

_____

_____

_____

_____

_____

Partner B

_____

_____

_____

_____

_____

_____

SPICING THINGS UP

Among the most satisfying aspects of a strong committed relation-ship are trust, safety, and security. But sometimes we can get stuck in patterns of sameness. In this exercise, let's use the trust between you and your partner to play with novelty and unpredictability to have an affair—with each other. Try role-playing with each other as complete strangers, with completely new personas. Enact it however you like, perhaps beginning with text and social media messages. Be flirtatious, curious, and playful as each of you tries to get to know this intriguing stranger you've just met. The goal is to see each other under the light of newness and rekindle the excite-ment of novelty.

What does the term *compatibility* mean to you? List several ways that you and your partner are compatible with each other. Then write down an incompatibility or two—every couple has them.

Partner A

_____

_____

_____

_____

_____

_____

Partner B

_____

_____

_____

_____

_____

_____

But let there be spaces in your togetherness and let the winds of the heavens dance between you. Love one another but make not a bond of love: let it rather be a moving sea between the shores of your souls.

KAHLIL GIBRAN, POET

FINDING BALANCE

Balancing your relationship with the forces that demand your attention in the outside world—obligations, work, social life, children, extended family, and so on—is challenging. Life is a balance—you don't want to lose yourself in your relationship. But you don't want to neglect your relationship because you have too much work, an upcoming activity, or needy friends. This exercise challenges you to have a heart-to-heart conversation about the concept of balance. Take turns asking each other the following questions, staying kind and curious as you see where the conversation takes you.

1. Is our relationship balanced?
2. What would perfect balance look like in different aspects of life?
3. Is there a part of your life you wish was more balanced?
4. How could you find more balance?
5. How can I help you find more balance?

A healthy relationship requires that you both have deep respect for your differences. This can be difficult—the bigger a difference, the harder it is to accept. What differences exist between your partner and you? What are the qualities, behaviors, and inclinations that each of you finds hardest to understand or relate to? Which do you fully accept, and which are harder to embrace?

Partner A

_____

_____

_____

_____

_____

_____

Partner B

_____

_____

_____

_____

_____

_____

_____

What does it mean for you to fully accept your partner with all their differences and flaws? Is there anything that you are tolerating instead of accepting? What would it look like for you to fully accept your partner as they are?

Partner A

_____

_____

_____

_____

_____

_____

Partner B

_____

_____

_____

_____

_____

_____

Establishing and respecting boundaries requires understanding, compassion, and communication. What boundaries exist in your relationship? Are there behaviors of your partner that you think require some boundary-setting (for example, excessive people-pleasing, being disrespectful, or trying to change you)? What new boundaries might be helpful?

Partner A

_____

_____

_____

_____

_____

Partner B

_____

_____

_____

_____

_____

_____

LIKES, NEEDS, AND DESIRES

Our personal needs and tastes are constantly evolving, which can create turbulence in a relationship if a couple is resistant to changes. This exercise asks you to define your past and present likes, needs, and desires to help you reflect on those changes.

Likes are things that you can live without but that are enjoyable to have, such as your favorite food or music.

Needs make you feel fulfilled and you consider them necessary for a satisfying life, such as exercise, social activities, and quiet time.

Desires are strong feelings of wanting to do something or wanting something to happen.

Over time, changes may shift from one category to another. Fill in the following table. Afterward, review and discuss.

Partner A			
	Likes	**Needs**	**Desires**
10 years ago			
5 years ago			
Today			

Partner B			
	Likes	**Needs**	**Desires**
10 years ago			
5 years ago			
Today			

There's a familiar saying: "If you love something, set it free." Giving your partner space to thrive as an individual can be difficult to do. But it's a must for establishing a healthy, balanced relationship. List your needs for personal time and space. How do you and your partner honor these? Have your needs changed over time?

Partner A

_____

_____

_____

_____

_____

_____

Partner B

_____

_____

_____

_____

_____

_____

Personal boundaries are the limits we put in place regarding how we want to be treated. They assure a relationship is mutually respectful and caring. Describe boundaries you have consciously or unconsciously set in your romantic relationship and other aspects of your life (family, work, friends).

Partner A

_____

_____

_____

_____

_____

_____

Partner B

_____

_____

_____

_____

_____

_____

Which of your own actions and behaviors could you change to be a better partner? Think about your needs and desires as a couple and as individuals. What would you like to say "yes" to more? What would you like to say "no" to more? What prevents you from doing so now?

Partner A

_____

_____

_____

_____

_____

_____

Partner B

_____

_____

_____

_____

_____

_____

In desperate love, we always invent the characters of our partners, demanding they be what we need of them, and then feeling devastated when they refuse to perform the role we created in the first place.

ELIZABETH GILBERT, AUTHOR

A loving, committed relationship can be ideal for encouraging and supporting each other's dreams. But it requires a significant amount of trust to open up about our dreams, not knowing if the other person will be supportive. Describe three or four of your biggest dreams, why each is important to you, and how your partner can help you realize them.

Partner A

_____

_____

_____

_____

_____

_____

Partner B

_____

_____

_____

_____

_____

_____

Kindness and compassion are important, sustaining practices that require intent—they don't just happen. When is it easiest for you to bring kindness and compassion to your relationship? What is the kindest and most compassionate thing you could do for yourself right now? For your partner?

Partner A

_____

_____

_____

_____

_____

_____

_____

Partner B

_____

_____

_____

_____

_____

_____

_____

LOVING KINDNESS MEDITATION

This exercise is designed to foster greater trust and awareness, and it's inspired by a mindfulness practice called loving kindness meditation. Here's how to do it:

1. Sit facing each other in a comfortable position and hold hands. Set a timer for at least two minutes.

2. Look into each other's eyes and don't speak; just stare at each other.

3. Bring awareness to your breathing, and try to synchronize it with your partner's.

4. Bring awareness to the places where your body is in contact with your partner's body.

5. Maintain eye contact and send loving thoughts. Try this traditional loving kindness blessing: "May you be safe, may you be healthy, may you be happy, may you live with ease, may you be loved." Or create your own.

6. If a distracting thought interrupts you, observe it, imagine it's a cloud that's drifting past, and go back to awareness of your breathing. Start again to send loving thoughts.

Describe what gives you strength in times of uncertainty. How can your partner be supportive when fears come up and you need to find that inner strength? How can you communicate those needs in the moment?

Partner A

_____

_____

_____

_____

_____

_____

_____

Partner B

_____

_____

_____

_____

_____

_____

_____

We learn how to deal with strong and uncomfortable emotions when we're young. How supportive of your emotions was your family when you were growing up? How did you learn to communicate those emotions? How comfortable are you sharing uncomfortable emotions today?

Partner A

_____

_____

_____

_____

_____

_____

Partner B

_____

_____

_____

_____

_____

_____

Stress brings out our fight-or-flight instincts. It can turn a pussycat into a bobcat. What are your behavioral tendencies when you're upset or emotionally disconnected? Do you become testy, defensive, or withdrawn? How can you join together to create a safe haven for sharing and working through strong emotions when one of you is stressed?

Partner A

_____

_____

_____

_____

_____

Partner B

_____

_____

_____

_____

_____

_____

It's when we're vulnerable that connection and closeness happen. But being vulnerable is not easy. What gets in the way of you being fully vulnerable with your partner? Do you fend off vulnerability with defensive behaviors like accusation, blame, criticism, or just shutting down?

Partner A

_____

_____

_____

_____

_____

_____

Partner B

_____

_____

_____

_____

_____

_____

Teamwork is key for a successful relationship. How can you become a better team player? What changes could you make to bring your best to the game?

Partner A

_____

_____

_____

_____

_____

_____

Partner B

_____

_____

_____

_____

_____

_____

_____

TEAMWORK

Pick a task that you have been mutually procrastinating on (for example, cleaning the garage, scheduling a dinner with friends, starting a new exercise routine, or detoxing from Netflix). Now work as a team to develop a plan to accomplish that task. Start by answering the following questions:

What is our goal and why is it important?

_____

_____

What steps do we need to follow, together and separately, to accomplish the goal?

_____

_____

_____

_____

What are the strengths and weaknesses each of us brings to the task?

_____

_____

_____

How can we make this fun?

_____

_____

_____

How will we celebrate when the task is completed?

_____

_____

_____

Whatever happens around you, don't take it personally. . . . Nothing other people do is because of you. It is because of themselves.

DON MIGUEL RUIZ,
SPIRITUAL TEACHER AND AUTHOR

3
CONFLICT

Although conflict is stressful, a relationship does require some conflict to grow. In this section, we will dive into this paradox and learn how to harness the power of conflict for a deeper, more intimate relationship. You will explore your negative interactions, identify and examine your triggers, and learn how to approach sensitive topics with curiosity instead of judgment. We will also consider techniques for handling conflict and the important role of forgiveness.

Think of recent times when you've been at odds with your partner, and describe the feelings and behaviors that came up. How do you tend to respond to conflict between the two of you? What do you think is the motivation for your response? For example, do you lose your temper because you want your opinion to be honored?

Partner A

_____

_____

_____

_____

_____

_____

Partner B

_____

_____

_____

_____

_____

_____

Describe what you think your partner needs or longs for during a negative skirmish.

Partner A

_____

_____

_____

_____

_____

_____

Partner B

_____

_____

_____

_____

_____

_____

How do you tend to communicate when you are under stress or feel negative emotions, such as anger, sadness, fear, frustration, or loneliness?

Partner A

_____

_____

_____

_____

_____

_____

_____

Partner B

_____

_____

_____

_____

_____

_____

_____

Would you like to be able to communicate differently during times of stress than you do now? How so?

Partner A

_____

_____

_____

_____

_____

_____

Partner B

_____

_____

_____

_____

_____

_____

PRACTICE NONVIOLENT COMMUNICATION

Developed by Marshall Rosenberg, nonviolent communication is a communication method focused on needs and on relating with compassion during a dispute. To try it, bring up a recent minor disagreement. Each of you take a turn making your case:

1. Share only the facts, as you understand them.

For example: "You said you'd pick me up, but by my accounting you were 45 minutes late."

2. Observe your feelings and communicate them.

For example: "I was frustrated, and worried that I wouldn't get to my nephew's school play on time."

3. Describe your unmet needs.

For example: "I really needed to know I could rely on you."

4. Make a request that would help resolve the issue in the future.

For example: "When you're running late, please keep me updated."

Conflict can bring up strong negative emotions, and it can be helpful to think of these emotions in terms of underlying fears. Think of a recent negative interaction with your partner, and write down the feelings you experienced. What could be the fear behind each feeling? For example, if you felt angry during an argument about your monthly budget, the underlying fear could be that you're not saving enough money and will end up in debt.

Partner A

_____

_____

_____

_____

_____

_____

Partner B

_____

_____

_____

_____

_____

When it comes to conflict, there are three negative cycles that couples might fall into:

- One person attacks, then the other counterattacks.

- One person makes a demand, then the other withdraws. The first person increases the intensity of the demand.

- Both withdraw emotionally from each other.

Do you fall into any of those patterns? Describe how conflict plays out.

Partner A

_____

_____

_____

_____

_____

Partner B

_____

_____

_____

_____

_____

As a child, what did you learn about expressing feelings of anger, fear, sadness, love, and affection? What methods did people in your home use to communicate their feelings? Were certain feelings more welcome than others? If writing about this topic brings up negative feelings, acknowledge them and tell your partner how they can support you.

Partner A

_____

_____

_____

_____

_____

_____

Partner B

_____

_____

_____

_____

_____

_____

_____

ARE YOU THERE FOR ME?

The big question that is the base of a healthy, trusting relationship is this: "Are you there for me?" If you know at your core that the answer is yes, then you have a good basis for overcoming any setbacks that life throws at the two of you. The questions in this exercise are designed to remind both of you that you are each other's best allies, and that you are there for each other.

1. Set aside some time when you won't be distracted, and sit comfortably together.

2. Look into each other's eyes.

3. Take turns asking and answering these questions:

- Is it easy to connect with me?
- How can I be more supportive when things get tough?
- Are there times when you feel misunderstood by me?
- How can I be a better listener?
- How can I show you that I accept you the way you are?

I often make the mistake of thinking that something that is obvious to me is just as obvious to everyone else.

CHIMAMANDA NGOZI ADICHIE,
AUTHOR AND MACARTHUR FELLOW

Emotional responsiveness—being accessible, responsive, and engaged with your partner—enables a relationship to overcome any obstacle. Describe a situation that challenged you in the last year. How did you cope with it? What did your partner do to make you feel supported? Was your partner as responsive to you as you needed?

Partner A

_____

_____

_____

_____

_____

_____

Partner B

_____

_____

_____

_____

_____

_____

ACCEPTING EACH OTHER

According to relationship researcher and author John Gottman, to address any kind of problem successfully, you need to communicate acceptance of who your partner is at their core. In other words, if a partner feels judged, misunderstood, or criticized, the problem won't be solved. For this exercise, each of you makes a list of all the things you love and accept about your partner. Take your time and include big things (like their commitment to this relationship) and little things (such as the way they clean the dishes after dinner). Then share your lists with each other. Save the lists so you can both read them after a negative interaction with each other. The less you feel like reading the list when you're angry or frustrated with your partner, the more you need to read it.

Recall moments in your relationship when you felt totally stress-free, at ease, and deeply connected with your partner. What were the circumstances? What do they have in common? How might you replicate these conditions on a regular basis?

Partner A

_____

_____

_____

_____

_____

_____

Partner B

_____

_____

_____

_____

_____

_____

A SAFE PLACE

Stress is our body's reaction to danger. This exercise teaches you to tap into feelings of safety to turn off the stress reaction.

1. Sit together in a relaxed position.
2. Each of you close your eyes and visualize a place, in your memory or imagination, where you feel safe and completely relaxed. Re-create what you feel in all your senses—for example, if you're on a beach, you'll feel the sun, smell the ocean, and hear the waves.
3. Stay in that place for a few minutes. When you are both ready, gently bring your attention back to your surroundings.

Share your safe haven with your partner, in as much detail as possible. Each of you should treat this information as sacred. Practice going to this place every day, together or separately, as your schedule allows. The next time you are in a stressful situation, go to your safe haven mentally.

Listening deeply is essential for repairing emotional damage. Recall a time when you felt truly listened to, either by your partner or by someone else. What were the circumstances? What cues—body language, eye contact, or verbal responses—made you feel you were being listened to? With that mind, how can you create a better environment for listening to your partner?

Partner A

_____

_____

_____

_____

_____

Partner B

_____

_____

_____

_____

_____

Think of a recent fight, disagreement, or conflict between the two of you. Then switch to your partner's perspective and document in detail what happened. Capture their reality by describing the sequence of events from their point of view: what they thought, how they felt, and what they needed.

Partner A

_____

_____

_____

_____

_____

_____

Partner B

_____

_____

_____

_____

_____

_____

_____

What are your triggers? A trigger can be anything that sparks intense negative emotions: a person, an event, a particular noise or smell, or even a sensitive topic like money, family, or sex. Describe at least three triggers and suggest how each might be linked to past negative experiences, and how your partner can be more understanding and supportive. Note: If there is underlying trauma connected to a trigger, look for professional help to heal it.

Partner A

_____

_____

_____

_____

_____

_____

Partner B

_____

_____

_____

_____

_____

_____

Therapist and author Harville Hendrix has said "Conflict is growth trying to happen." How can conflict help each of you grow as a person, and grow together as a couple? Can you think of times in the past when this kind of growth happened?

Partner A

_____

_____

_____

_____

_____

_____

Partner B

_____

_____

_____

_____

_____

_____

For a relationship to be successful, partners need to have a healthy connection. Taking care to nurture this connection must be a priority. What does a healthy connection mean to you? What are some signals that your connection to your partner is healthy and strong?

Partner A

_____

_____

_____

_____

_____

_____

Partner B

_____

_____

_____

_____

_____

_____

How can you strengthen your connection with your partner? Brainstorm and list everything that comes to your mind, even if it sounds ridiculous or silly (e.g., "leave loving sticky notes in strange places," "finish the project that you promised you would a while ago," "block out 10 minutes every day for checking in").

Partner A

_____

_____

_____

_____

_____

_____

Partner B

_____

_____

_____

_____

_____

_____

Describe an unresolved conflict in your relationship or in your life. Why do you think it hasn't been resolved? Is there anything you could have done in the moment that would have produced a different outcome? Is this something you would like to resolve now? How would that feel?

Partner A

_____

_____

_____

_____

_____

_____

Partner B

_____

_____

_____

_____

_____

_____

MINDFULNESS BREAK

When concerns about the future and the past feel overwhelming, it's time to focus on the present moment by taking a mindfulness break. You can employ mindfulness while doing whatever task is at hand.

1. Focus on the present moment as much as you can. Start by becoming aware of your breathing, paying attention to each inhale and exhale.
2. Attend to the sensations that you're experiencing, whether it's the feeling of your body in the chair as you meditate, or the smell of grass and noise of the mower as you cut your lawn.
3. If your mind wanders from the present, gently focus on what you're doing or focus on your breath. When feelings come up, positive or negative, just acknowledge them, without judgment.

You can try this practice separately or together. Afterward, talk to each other about how it went. Try to replicate this mindful awareness the next time a conflict arises.

Are you holding on to negative thoughts, feelings, or behaviors (e.g., anxiety, anger, a need to control, rigidity, assumptions, judgments) that harm your relationship? How would your relationship improve if you were able to let go of those things?

Partner A

_____

_____

_____

_____

_____

_____

Partner B

_____

_____

_____

_____

_____

_____

What does forgiveness mean to you? Describe a time in your life when you received a wholehearted apology from someone who wronged you. Were you able to forgive?

Partner A

_____

_____

_____

_____

_____

_____

_____

Partner B

_____

_____

_____

_____

_____

_____

_____

Psychologist Sue Johnson has said, "The most functional way to regulate difficult emotions in love relationships is to share them." Describe an interaction with your partner that triggered a difficult emotion in you. Write the thoughts, feelings, and needs that accompanied this emotion. How can your partner help you process those emotions next time?

Partner A

_____

_____

_____

_____

_____

_____

Partner B

_____

_____

_____

_____

_____

_____

_____

Think of the most recent, or most intense, argument or regrettable incident between you and your partner. What part of it are you accountable for?

Partner A

_____

_____

_____

_____

_____

_____

Partner B

_____

_____

_____

_____

_____

_____

_____

SAYING I'M SORRY

Apologizing isn't always easy, but it can become easier with practice. For this exercise, begin by asking your partner about something you did that really hurt their feelings. Listen to what they have to say about it. Then write a heartfelt apology letter including the following elements:

Remorse: Express unequivocal regret for the hurt you caused.

Accountability: Take full responsibility for your actions.

Validation: Validate your partner's feelings by acknowledging that they were hurt.

Action: Commit to an action you will take moving forward—either a reparation or a step you're taking so this won't happen again.

When you are finished, get together with your partner and read the letter out loud. Note that this doesn't require anything from your partner. Forgiveness is optional.

When you're ready, reverse roles and repeat.

Part of peace-making is acknowledging that we can't know everything about ourselves, and sometimes we reveal things to others that we are not ready to accept.

SARAH SCHULMAN,
ACTIVIST, WRITER, AND HISTORIAN

The past is never dead. It's not even past.

WILLIAM FAULKNER,
NOBEL AND PULITZER PRIZE–WINNING AUTHOR

4
FAMILY MATTERS

Our past relationships and upbringing are integral to the way we behave as a partner in an adult relationship. In this section, we will dig into your past to explore what behavioral patterns, emotional baggage, values, and beliefs you have brought from your childhood to your life today. Through these journal prompts, you will take a close look at the impact of your family relationships and family history on your current relationship. You will explore your thoughts and beliefs about very personal matters, explore grief and loss in your lives, and discover how to support each other.

Describe what it was like to grow up in your family. Reflect on what was good or bad, safe or scary, sad or happy.

Partner A

_____

_____

_____

_____

_____

_____

Partner B

_____

_____

_____

_____

_____

_____

What events or circumstances of your childhood influenced how you feel about yourself today? Can you relate any of your current behaviors to an event or situation in your past?

Partner A

_____

_____

_____

_____

_____

_____

_____

Partner B

_____

_____

_____

_____

_____

_____

_____

BUILDING UP RESILIENCE

For this practice, get together at a time when you can have a relaxed conversation with each other. Each of you pick a struggle from your past—it might be something you had to overcome as a child or something you conquered more recently. Briefly describe what happened, then answer these questions:

- What personal strengths did you use to overcome the issue?
- Who helped you?
- What did it mean for you to leave that struggle behind?
- How did your life change?
- Would you do anything differently if you could?

Be sure that both of you get the opportunity to tell your story.

If you could go back to your childhood, how would you behave or interact differently with your family? Why?

Partner A

_____

_____

_____

_____

_____

_____

Partner B

_____

_____

_____

_____

_____

_____

Never regret your past. Rather, embrace it as the teacher that it is.

ROBIN SHARMA,
AUTHOR AND LEADERSHIP EXPERT

Describe how positive and negative feelings were dealt with in your family.
Were you encouraged to express your emotions? Were you judged because of
your feelings?

Partner A

_____

_____

_____

_____

_____

_____

_____

Partner B

_____

_____

_____

_____

_____

_____

_____

HOUSEHOLD MEETING

For this exercise, make a plan with you partner to hold a weekly household meeting. If there are children in your family, they might be included. The purpose is to create a safe space in which everybody can have open communication. Choose the best time and setting for the first meeting, decide on the rules, and put it on everyone's calendar. The structure is up to you, but everybody attending should have an opportunity to speak on the subjects at hand without being interrupted. Set a pattern at your first meeting and adjust it as needed. The good and the bad should be brought up. Celebrate successes, cooperate to solve problems, establish and adjust rules, and share feelings without judgment.

How have the adult relationships that you observed as a child, and the behaviors and coping mechanisms you learned, affected the way you act and react in your relationship with your partner?

Partner A

_____

_____

_____

_____

_____

_____

Partner B

_____

_____

_____

_____

_____

_____

How supportive is your family of your relationship? Does your family, or your partner's family, ever get in the way of your relationship? How so?

Partner A

_____

_____

_____

_____

_____

_____

Partner B

_____

_____

_____

_____

_____

_____

It's easy to get caught up in responsibilities and commitments outside your relationship. What boundaries would you like to set regarding others' demands on your time to make sure your partner feels like a priority in your life? Try to list at least four. (Example: *I don't check work emails after 7 p.m.*)

Partner A

_____

_____

_____

_____

_____

_____

Partner B

_____

_____

_____

_____

_____

_____

"It's us against the world." Describe what comes to mind when you consider that statement. Can you think of recent examples when you've put the concept into practice?

Partner A

_____

_____

_____

_____

_____

_____

Partner B

_____

_____

_____

_____

_____

_____

US FIRST

In this exercise, you'll write a contract in which both of you commit to putting your relationship first, by agreeing on how and when to make room for outside disruptions.

Begin by discussing the key components that you want to include in your contract. How often will you welcome other people or activities into your life? What happens when outside obligations take up too much time?

Be as general or specific as you like. Some examples of how you might address these issues:

- "We commit to prioritizing quality time together by . . ."
- "Any overnight guest needs to give two weeks' notice, and we need to discuss it with each other before agreeing."
- "We will tell each other first whenever there is something important to share."

When you've come to an agreement on all points, write out your contract, sign it, and seal it with a kiss. Store the document where you can review the details when you need to.

Do you ever find that maintaining two relationships, one with your family and the other with your partner, puts you in a difficult position? If so, describe what happened and how that made you feel. If not, how do you successfully balance the different relationships?

Partner A

_____

_____

_____

_____

_____

_____

_____

Partner B

_____

_____

_____

_____

_____

_____

_____

What values (principles that are important to you) that you learned as a child do you still retain today? What new values have you added to your life? What common values do you share with your partner?

Partner A

_____

_____

_____

_____

_____

_____

_____

Partner B

_____

_____

_____

_____

_____

_____

_____

Not every couple is concerned with having children. But for those who consider it, becoming a parent is probably the most important decision you will make in your life. What are your thoughts about having children? What is most scary about the idea? What is most exciting?

Partner A

_____

_____

_____

_____

_____

_____

Partner B

_____

_____

_____

_____

_____

_____

How would your resources (time, money, health, work) be affected if you added a child to your family? How do you feel about that? Is your relationship with your partner solid enough, or serious enough, to add a child at this time?

Partner A

_____

_____

_____

_____

_____

_____

_____

Partner B

_____

_____

_____

_____

_____

_____

_____

If you envision having children at some point, how many children would you like to have? Describe how set you are on that number, and why it's important for you. If you have already reached your ideal number, or don't want to have children, describe why that is the case.

Partner A

_____

_____

_____

_____

_____

_____

_____

Partner B

_____

_____

_____

_____

_____

_____

_____

How do you think having a child would change your life? How do you think your romantic relationship would change?

Partner A

_____

_____

_____

_____

_____

_____

_____

Partner B

_____

_____

_____

_____

_____

_____

_____

What do you think are the most important values you would like to pass on to your children, or to the next generation (nieces and nephews, friends' children, etc.)? Why are they important to you?

Partner A

_____

_____

_____

_____

_____

_____

Partner B

_____

_____

_____

_____

_____

_____

LIFE IS A LESSON

We've all had defining experiences that teach us important lessons. Being open to these life lessons is a great way to grow as a person, and a benefit of being in a relationship is that your life lessons can be shared. Even if you haven't lived the same experiences as your partner, you still can learn from them.

Sit with your partner and ask each other the following questions:

- What's the biggest life lesson you would like to pass on to the next generation, if you had the chance?
- What is your biggest lesson about relationships?
- Give an example of how a life lesson that you've learned recently could have helped you in the past.
- How can we be more open to learning every day?

Describe your ideal way of dealing with conflict between family members.
What's your biggest strength when dealing with family conflict? What's your biggest weakness?

Partner A

_____

_____

_____

_____

_____

_____

Partner B

_____

_____

_____

_____

_____

_____

What is the most important responsibility a parent has toward their children?
What parenting style (e.g., supportive, strict, encouraging, relaxed) do you most
admire, and why?

Partner A

_____

_____

_____

_____

_____

_____

_____

Partner B

_____

_____

_____

_____

_____

_____

_____

Were you raised in the parenting style you admire? What would you take from the way you were raised, and why?

Partner A

_____

_____

_____

_____

_____

_____

Partner B

_____

_____

_____

_____

_____

_____

A broken family is a family in which any member must break herself into pieces to fit in. A whole family is one in which each member can bring her full self to the table knowing that she will always be both held and free.

GLENNON DOYLE, AUTHOR

IN OUR HOME, WE BELIEVE . . .

To celebrate and strengthen your shared convictions, create your own "family rules" poster.

1. Brainstorm and list as many ideas as you can think of. Your rules can be serious ("Kindness is everything"), fun ("Puppies are cute"), or a mix.

2. Discuss each statement, and refine the list until you have a list of principles everyone agrees with and that reflects the personality of the family.

3. Create your sign using paper, poster board, or other materials. Label it at the top: "In this family (or house, or whatever you prefer), we believe in:"

4. Post your sign where everyone will see it frequently.

Describe how you tend to react and cope with grief and loss, and how that differs from your partner.

Partner A

_____

_____

_____

_____

_____

_____

_____

Partner B

_____

_____

_____

_____

_____

_____

_____

What is the worst thing that has ever happened to you in your life? How did you deal with it?

Partner A

_____

_____

_____

_____

_____

_____

Partner B

_____

_____

_____

_____

_____

_____

What are some ways that you can support your partner when loss or hardship happens? How would you like your partner to support you?

Partner A

_____

_____

_____

_____

_____

_____

Partner B

_____

_____

_____

_____

_____

_____

When you are dealing with hardship, how do you turn toward your partner? How do they show up for you?

Partner A

_____

_____

_____

_____

_____

_____

Partner B

_____

_____

_____

_____

_____

_____

PLANNING FOR THE WORST

Adversity, pain, and loss are inevitable. To help each other prepare for the unexpected, plan a meeting—or a series of meetings—when you can discuss strategies to enable you to be there for each other.

Some points to talk over:

- How have each of you dealt with grief in the past? Do you tend to reach out to loved ones or to isolate?

- What's the plan if one of you dies or is significantly disabled? Do you have a will and other legal contingencies in place? If not, what are the steps to get that done?

- What happens if a close family member needs assistance, or if one of you loses their job? What other financial challenges should you be prepared for?

If you want to get detailed, you can create documents outlining the steps to take in various scenarios, so when the time comes it will be easier to make decisions.

Intimacy is the capacity to be rather weird with someone—and finding that that's OK with them.

ALAIN DE BOTTON, AUTHOR

5
SEX AND INTIMACY

Sex, intimacy, and affection deepen the feelings of connection in any relationship. But for many of us, these are not easy topics to discuss, especially during times of stress. The quotes, prompts, and practices in this final portion of the journal will help you and your partner open up and explore your inner landscapes, sharing insights about sexuality, desires, intimacy, eroticism, love languages, and intimate connection. And you'll have fun in the process.

Complete this sentence, sharing at least five examples:
"I feel most loved by my partner when . . ."

Partner A

_____

_____

_____

_____

_____

_____

Partner B

_____

_____

_____

_____

_____

_____

Feeling appreciated for who you are and what you do is indispensable for a happy relationship. Describe five things you most appreciate about your partner's personality, and name five specific things they've done that you're grateful for.

Partner A

_____

_____

_____

_____

_____

_____

_____

Partner B

_____

_____

_____

_____

_____

_____

_____

What actions could you start taking today to make sure your partner never feels taken for granted? Name at least three.

Partner A

_____

_____

_____

_____

_____

_____

Partner B

_____

_____

_____

_____

_____

_____

What is your favorite way of being appreciated? What could your partner do for you to feel loved and appreciated in that way? Give five examples or more.

Partner A

_____

_____

_____

_____

_____

_____

_____

Partner B

_____

_____

_____

_____

_____

_____

_____

SPEAKING IN LOVE LANGUAGES

We all have a preferred way to express and receive love—what author Gary Chapman describes as a "love language." From the following list, each of you choose your favorite ways to receive love. Ask yourself, "Which of these ways makes me feel the most loved by and connected to my partner?"

Acts of service: My partner does things that they know I like, or that make my life easier.

Gift giving: My partner surprises me with thoughtful tokens or presents.

Quality time: We spend time together in a meaningful way.

Physical touch: We hold hands, cuddle, and hug.

Words of affirmation: My partner says things that make me feel loved and appreciated.

After you identify each other's love language, make a list together, with at least 10 ideas of how each of you can speak the other person's love language.

Imagination is a powerful tool for exploring and expressing your desires. Use the space provided to write a sexy, spicy short scene, in first person, with you and your partner as the protagonists. For example, you might start, "It was a hot, sweaty afternoon and as I was lying in bed trying to fall asleep . . ."

Partner A

_____

_____

_____

_____

_____

_____

Partner B

_____

_____

_____

_____

_____

_____

Finish this sentence: "My favorite way that my partner initiates sex is when . . ."

Partner A

_____

_____

_____

_____

_____

_____

_____

_____

Partner B

_____

_____

_____

_____

_____

_____

_____

_____

Finish this sentence: "The best way for my partner to decline sex is by . . ."

Partner A

_____

_____

_____

_____

_____

_____

_____

Partner B

_____

_____

_____

_____

_____

_____

_____

LET'S HAVE FUN

Playing and laughing together reduce stress, and having fun can be a great awakener of erotic energy. When you were dating, you and your partner made it a point to do fun things together, which increased your attraction to each other. Set up an evening when work and other responsibilities will be put aside, and you can play some fun games.

Come up with activities that will lower your inhibitions with some playful, romantic, or spicy challenges. For example:

- Strip poker
- Karaoke night (love songs only)
- The jar of desire: Each partner writes out 10 sexy questions or actions, and the other picks out one to perform or answer

Describe what sex means and what intimacy means for you. How are they different?

Partner A

_____

_____

_____

_____

_____

_____

Partner B

_____

_____

_____

_____

_____

_____

_____

When have you felt your most authentic sexual self, whatever that may mean for you? Describe what that felt like.

Partner A

_____

_____

_____

_____

_____

_____

_____

Partner B

_____

_____

_____

_____

_____

_____

_____

How were sex and sexuality discussed in your home growing up? What messages or ideas about sex have you learned in the past that have shaped the way you think about and experience it now?

Partner A

_____

_____

_____

_____

_____

_____

Partner B

_____

_____

_____

_____

_____

_____

Psychologist Esther Perel talks about the basic human needs of security and novelty. As a relationship progresses and security increases, often the novelty will decrease. What are some ways in which your relationship helps you feel secure? What aspects of your relationship no longer feel novel? What are some ways to add novelty and spark into your relationship?

Partner A

_____

_____

_____

_____

_____

_____

Partner B

_____

_____

_____

_____

_____

_____

SEXY SEXTING

A great way to spark flirting and share intimate thoughts is via text messages. Find this out for yourself by using what you've learned about what turns your partner on to start a sexy, playful text thread. This activity also builds anticipation for being together in person, which increases desire. Flip a coin to decide who will start the text, at a time of their choosing, when you're apart. Let the conversation develop as you text back and forth over the course of a few hours or days . . . not for too long, so the intensity won't fade.

Besides sex, what kind of activities can you do together to feel more intimacy and connection in your relationship?

Partner A

_____

_____

_____

_____

_____

_____

_____

Partner B

_____

_____

_____

_____

_____

_____

_____

Emotional intimacy is that feeling of closeness in a relationship that helps break down personal barriers. What's going on in your life right now that affects your emotional intimacy, for good or ill? Reflect on the things that contribute to your capacity for emotional intimacy.

Partner A

_____

_____

_____

_____

_____

_____

Partner B

_____

_____

_____

_____

_____

_____

Is there anything preventing you from deepening your sexual connection with your partner? What obstacles can you work on together? Here are some examples: body insecurities, unspoken fears, life stressors, medical problems, mental health issues, religious or social taboos, or differences in desire.

Partner A

_____

_____

_____

_____

_____

_____

Partner B

_____

_____

_____

_____

_____

_____

Describe where you are right now in your life regarding sexual desire. What are your needs now, and how have they changed over time?

Partner A

_____

_____

_____

_____

_____

_____

Partner B

_____

_____

_____

_____

_____

_____

AWAKENING SENSUALITY

Merriam-Webster.com defines sensuality as "relating to or consisting in the gratification of the senses or the indulgence of appetite." Sensuality is, in other words, the enjoyment of pleasures, including sex, through our senses. Often that means we need to get out of our heads and get in touch with our bodies, and that's the idea behind this exercise. Follow these guidelines:

1. Plan an occasion when the two of you can spend time together and stimulate every sense. Enjoy delicious food, put on inspiring music, warm some fragrant essential oils, light some candles, or turn the lights down and give each other a massage or simply caress each other.

2. Savor each sensory experience, and when you notice that your thoughts are taking over, go back to the senses and the pleasure.

3. Do not do this exercise with expectations of having sex, but simply enjoy the sensual pleasures as the end goal.

What factors contribute to you feeling sexy and in the mood? List as many as you can think of, including external factors (like being away from home, getting to bed early, having a date night, seeing your partner nicely dressed and groomed), and internal ones (like feeling rested and relaxed, feeling good about your body).

Partner A

_____

_____

_____

_____

_____

_____

Partner B

_____

_____

_____

_____

_____

_____

To be sensual, I think, is to respect and rejoice in the force of life, of life itself, and to be present in all that one does, from the effort of loving to the breaking of bread.

JAMES BALDWIN,
NOVELIST, ESSAYIST, AND PLAYWRIGHT

Knowing what excites each other physically is important for a couple's satisfactory sex life. Make a list of the things that turn you on. Think of all the things that make you feel fully alive: for example, getting a massage, feeling the sun warming up your skin on a winter day, or feeling desired by your partner.

Partner A

_____

_____

_____

_____

_____

Partner B

_____

_____

_____

_____

_____

Esther Perel says that "the central agent of eroticism is our imaginations." What does that statement mean to you? Write down all the ways you might reconnect with your imagination in order to spark your sex life.

Partner A

_____

_____

_____

_____

_____

_____

_____

Partner B

_____

_____

_____

_____

_____

_____

_____

Fantasies are a key part of imagination. Write down a sexual fantasy you feel comfortable sharing with your partner.

Partner A

_____

_____

_____

_____

_____

_____

Partner B

_____

_____

_____

_____

_____

_____

ROLE-PLAYING

In this activity, let fantasy and imagination take over. This is about each of you pretending to be someone else and having fun with it. Discuss the possibilities and pick a scenario to enact, at home or in whatever setting you choose. If either of you feels a bit inhibited, open up and share that with your partner. Reassure each other that this is a safe game that's meant to be fun.

Here are a few suggestions:

- You're strangers who meet on a Caribbean island in an exclusive resort. Introduce yourselves to each other and explain what brings you there.

- The plane you both were traveling on has to make an emergency stop. You're stranded with no communication for the night. You've never met before.

- You both won a dinner at five-star restaurant. You don't know each other, but there has been a mistake and the maître d' seats you at the same table. What happens next?

What does a satisfactory sex life mean to you? What does it look like? How can you make having a satisfactory sex life a priority? What do you feel when you think about this topic?

Partner A

_____

_____

_____

_____

_____

_____

_____

Partner B

_____

_____

_____

_____

_____

_____

_____

What is the best part about sex for you?

Partner A

_____

_____

_____

_____

_____

_____

_____

Partner B

_____

_____

_____

_____

_____

_____

_____

EVERYTHING IS FOREPLAY

Couples therapy guru John Gottman's wisdom tells us that "Every positive thing you do in your relationship is foreplay." Put this wisdom into practice by choosing a day when you'll live by this precept. Spend that day doing positive things for each other. Possibilities include making the other person breakfast, saying thank you with a smile, sending nice and loving text messages, reminding your partner what you find physically attractive about them, or complimenting something they say or do. At the end of the day, discuss whether you feel more connected, emotionally and physically. Share how it felt for each of you to be doing nice things for the other. Does it seem like you increased your connection?

To truly experience sexual freedom, you must reclaim your erotic imagination and allow yourself to make your sex life a work of art, your very own creation designed to fulfill your unique needs and desires.

CHRIS MAXWELL ROSE,
SEX AND RELATIONSHIP COACH

A Final Word

Congratulations on taking this journey together. Being in a relationship is so rewarding, but the care and feeding of your relationship requires effort and commitment. By working through the pages of this book, you have shown to yourself and your partner that you are committed to each other. I hope that each of you has found that your eyes and your mind have been opened to new ways of seeing your partner as a lover and a best friend.

The process of journaling—commemorating your thoughts, feelings, and ideas on paper—provides a powerful way to unearth, develop, and share your thoughts, hopes, and dreams. If you've found that journaling with this book worked well for you, don't stop here. Keep writing; it can be such a fulfilling way to communicate. And now that you have worked together on opening the lines of communication, you don't have to begin these discussions with written words on a page. You can share with your partner in so many different ways: for example, send pictures or text messages, leave notes, or strike up a conversation in the car or at the breakfast table. You've seen what communication can do for your relationship. Use what you've learned here, and explore further with whatever methods work for you.

Every relationship has its ups and downs, its calm and its storms. But if you and your partner tend to the connection between you, together you'll keep learning, growing, and striving. And that makes life worthwhile!

Resources

Websites for Finding a Therapist

EMDR International Association, to find therapists specialized in trauma: EMDRIA.org/directory

Inclusive Therapists: Therapist directory with an emphasis on underserved communities and people with historically marginalized identities. InclusiveTherapists.com

MyWellBeing therapy matching service: MyWellbeing.com

Open Path Psychotherapy Collective, affordable counseling for those with financial need: OpenPathCollective.org

Psychology Today's "Find A Therapist" search tool: PsychologyToday.com/us/therapists

The Therapy Den, a national platform for therapists: TherapyDen.com

Blogs

Psychotherapist and author Esther Perel: EstherPerel.com/blog

Gottman Institute: Gottman.com/blog

Books

Happy Together: Using the Science of Positive Psychology to Build Love That Lasts by Suzann Pileggi Pawelski, MAPP, and James O. Pawelski, PhD

Hold Me Tight: Seven Conversations for a Lifetime of Love by Sue Johnson, EdD

Relationship Questions for Couples: Guided Conversations to Cultivate Curiosity, Communication, and Connection by Miriam Torres Brinkmann, PhD, LMFT

The Seven Principles for Making Marriage Work: A Practical Guide from the Country's Foremost Relationship Expert by John M. Gottman, PhD, and Nan Silver

The Ultimate Relationship Workbook for Couples: Simple Exercises to Improve Communication and Strengthen Your Bond by Ari Sytner

Podcasts

The Couples Therapist Couch with Hedy Schleifer

Speaking of Sex with the Pleasure Mechanics with Chris Maxwell Rose and Charlotte Mia Rose

Where Should We Begin with Esther Perel

References

Adichie, Chimamanda Ngozi. *We Should All Be Feminists*. New York: Vintage, 2014.

Baldwin, James. *The Fire Next Time*. New York: Vintage, 2013.

Bennett, Roy T. *The Light in the Heart: Inspirational Thoughts for Living Your Best Life*. Self-published, 2020.

Brown, Brené. *The Gifts of Imperfection: Let Go of Who You Think You're Supposed to Be and Embrace Who You Are*. Center City, MN: Hazelden Publishing, 2010.

Chapman, Gary. *The Five Love Languages: How to Express Heartfelt Commitment to Your Love*. Chicago: Northfield, 1995.

Culpepper, Jetta Carol. "Merriam-Webster Online: The Language Center." *Electronic Resources Review* 4, no. 1/2 (January 2000): 9–11. doi.org/10.1108/err.2000.4.1_2.9.11.

de Botton, Alain. *The Course of Love: A Novel*. New York: Simon & Schuster, 2016.

Doyle, Glennon. *Untamed*. New York: The Dial Press, 2020.

Faulkner, William. *Requiem for a Nun*. New York: Vintage, 2011.

Gibran, Kahlil. *The Prophet*. New York: Alfred A. Knopf, 1923.

Gilbert, Elizabeth. *Eat, Pray, Love: One Woman's Search for Everything*. London: A&C Black, 2007.

Gottman, John M. *The Science of Trust: Emotional Attunement for Couples*. New York: W. W. Norton & Company, 2011.

Gottman, John M., and Nan Silver. *The Seven Principles for Making Marriage Work: A Practical Guide from the Country's Foremost Relationship Expert*. New York: Harmony, 2015.

Gottman, John, Julie Schwartz Gottman, Doug Abrams, and Rachel Carlton Abrams. *The Man's Guide to Women: Scientifically Proven Secrets from the "Love Lab" About What Women Really Want*. New York: Rodale, 2016.

Gottman, John. "Building a Great Sex Life Is Not Rocket Science." Published January 4, 2017. *The Gottman Institute Blog.* Gottman.com/blog/building-great-sex-life-not -rocket-science.

Hendrix, Harville, and Helen Lakelly Hunt. "A New Way to Think about Couples." Keynote speech presented at the Couples Conference 2015, Manhattan Beach, CA, April 24, 2015.

Johnson, Sue. *Love Sense: The Revolutionary New Science of Romantic Relationships*. New York: Little, Brown Spark, 2013.

Keen, Sam. *To Love and Be Loved*. New York: Bantam Books, 1999.

Larsen, Kate. "The Power of Journaling: Written Reflections Help You to Gain Perspective on Your Past and to Maximize Your Future." *IDEA Fitness Journal* 3, no. 4 (April 2006): 94–97.

Lerner, Harriet. *Why Won't You Apologize?: Healing Big Betrayals and Everyday Hurts*. New York: Simon & Schuster, 2017.

Maxwell, Chris Rose, and Charlotte Mia Rose. *The Fantasy Method: How to Discover Your Authentic Sexual Desires and Create a Fulfilling Sex Life*. Self-published, 2012.

Osgarby, S. M., and W. K. Halford. "Couple Relationship Distress and Observed Expression of Intimacy During Reminiscence about Positive Relationship Events." *Behavior Therapy* 44, no. 4 (2013) 686–700. doi: 10.1016/j.beth.2013.05.003.

Pennebaker, James W., and Cindy K. Chung. "Expressive Writing: Connections to Physical and Mental Health." *The Oxford Handbook of Health Psychology*, August 2011. doi:10.1093/oxfordhb/9780195342819.013.0018.

Perel, Esther. "Bringing Home the Erotic: 5 Ways to Create Meaningful Connections with Your Partner." Esther Perel's blog. Accessed November 17, 2021. EstherPerel.com /blog/5-ways-to-create-meaningful-connections.

Perel, Esther. *Mating in Captivity: Unlocking Erotic Intelligence*. New York: Harper, 2007.

Rosenberg, Marshall B. *Nonviolent Communication: A Language of Life: Life-changing Tools for Healthy Relationships*. Encinitas, CA: PuddleDancer Press, 2015.

Ruiz, Don Miguel. *The Four Agreements: A Practical Guide to Personal Freedom*. San Rafael, CA: Amber-Allen Publishing, 1997.

Schulman, Sarah. *Conflict Is Not Abuse: Overstating Harm, Community Responsibility, and the Duty of Repair*. Vancouver: Arsenal Pulp Press, 2016.

Sharma, Robin. *The Monk Who Sold His Ferrari: A Fable About Fulfilling Your Dreams and Reaching Your Destiny*. Mumbai: Jaico Publishing House, 2003.

Tilley, Douglas, and Gail Palmer. "Enactments in Emotionally Focused Couple Therapy: Shaping Moments of Contact and Change." *Journal of Marital and Family Therapy* 39, no. 3 (July 2013): 299–313. doi.org/10.1111/j.1752-0606.2012.00305.x.

Ury, Logan. *How to Not Die Alone: The Surprising Science That Will Help You Find Love*. New York: Simon & Schuster, 2021.

Acknowledgments

First and foremost, I want to thank my husband, Peter Isler. Without him, this book wouldn't be possible. You are a true partner in crime.

My appreciation to Callisto Media, for trusting me, once again, and especially to my editor, Nora Spiegel.

To some of the people who really helped me be the therapist I am today: John and Julie Gottman, Ellyn Baden and Peter Pearson, Esther Perel, Sue Johnson, and many more. Their research, teachings, and inspiration are a never-ending source of wisdom.

All my great and beautiful amigas, here and there. I'm truly lucky for having you all in my life. Thank you for celebrating my achievements and for making my life much more fun.

Last but not a bit least, to all my clients. In session or afterward, they open their hearts and allow me to help them have better relationships.

About the Author

 **Miriam Torres Brinkmann, PhD, LMFT,** has a doctorate in psychology and a master's degree in marriage and family therapy. She has completed advanced training in the Gottman method, emotionally focused therapy, the developmental model of couples therapy, and eye movement desensitization and reprocessing (EMDR). She is also a mindfulness, wellness, and somatic coach; an associated certified coach; and a clinical hypnotherapist. Apart from her private online practice as a couples therapist and relationship coach, Miriam consults with clients as a life coach and conducts workshops in both English and Spanish for couples and individuals in different parts of the world. Her career is devoted to helping couples and individuals achieve flourishing relationships and live their best possible lives. Learn more at BrinkmannCenter.com.

CPSIA information can be obtained
at www.ICGtesting.com
Printed in the USA
JSHW012200150322
23882JS00001B/1